14.95

D1243455

Verbs in Action
Dig In

CSCL

Dana Meachen Rau

Marshall Cavendish
Benchmark
New York

2

Digging in the sand is a fun way to spend a day at the beach.

You can dig a deep hole with a shovel and pail. Your hands make good digging tools, too.

A gardener digs holes in soil. She plants seeds that will grow into plants. She uses a small shovel called a *trowel*.

People also dig to find things.

At a dinosaur dig, scientists search for *fossils*. The fossils are from dinosaurs that lived long ago.

8

Scientists dig into hard rock. They use small hammers, *chisels*, and brushes instead of shovels.

Big digging machines clear the way for a new building or road.

A *backhoe* has a claw at the end of a long arm. The claw can dig dirt and move it from place to place.

Some machines are built to dig through rock. They are used to dig *tunnels* for cars and trains to pass through.

13

People and machines do not just dig in dirt or sand. A farmer uses a *pitchfork* to dig through hay.

A snowplow digs snow. It clears the street so cars can pass safely.

Some animals live their whole lives digging underground. A mole has paws shaped like little scoops to dig the soil.

Earthworms eat the soil as
they dig through it. Moles and
earthworms dig all day long!

Animals also dig to look for food. An armadillo digs with its claws to look for insects.

Squirrels dig to save food for later. They dig little holes to bury acorns in.

Animals also dig to make tunnels to live in. The tunnels of an ant *colony* can get very crowded!

Chipmunks and woodchucks
dig tunnels, too.

They even dig rooms at the end of the tunnels, like underground houses.

"Dig" can also mean to look for something.

If you like to learn about space, you might go to a library to "dig up" books about rockets.

When you dig, you scoop something out to make a hole.

There is a meal on the table. You do not have a shovel. But you do have a spoon. You are ready to dig in!

Challenge Words

backhoe (BAK-ho)—A type of tractor with a claw at the end of a long arm for digging.

chisels (CHIZ-uhls)—Tools used to chip away hard rock or wood.

colony (KOL-uh-nee)—A group of animals living together.

fossils (FOS-uhls)—The hard parts left behind from dinosaurs long ago.

pitchfork (PICH-fork)—A tool a farmer uses to move hay.

trowel (TROW-uhl)—A small shovel used for planting.

tunnels (TUN-uhls)—Holes through mountains or the ground for cars, trains, or animals to pass through.

Index

Page numbers in **boldface** are illustrations.

With thanks to Nanci Vargus, Ed.D. and Beth Walker Gambro, reading consultants

Marshall Cavendish Benchmark
Marshall Cavendish
99 White Plains Road
Tarrytown, New York 10591-9001
www.marshallcavendish.us

Library of Congress Cataloging-in-Publication Data

Rau, Dana Meachen, 1971–
Dig in / by Dana Meachen Rau.
p. cm. — (Bookworms. Verbs in action)
Includes index.
ISBN 0-7614-1937-3
1. Dig (The English word)—Juvenile literature. 2. English language—Verb—Juvenile literature.
I. Title II. Series: Rau, Dana Meachen, 1971– .
Bookworms. Verbs in action.

PE1317.D54R388 2005
428.1—dc22
2004023400

Photo Research by Anne Burns Images

Cover photo: SuperStock/Robert Llewellyn

The photographs in this book are used with permission and through the courtesy of: *Photri*: pp. 1, 8, 11, 14, 15, 29.
SuperStock: p. 2 Kwame Zikomo. *Corbis*: p. 5 Ariel Skelley; p. 7 Tom Bean; p. 10 Lester Leftkowitz;
p. 13 Terres Du Sud; p. 16 James de Bounevialle/Cordaly Photo Library, Ltd.; p. 26 O'Brien Productions.
Animals Animals: pp. 17, 24; p. 19 Fred Whitehead; p. 20 OSF/Shay, A.; p. 23 OSF/Clyne, D.;
p. 25 Leonard Rue Enterprise.

Series design by Becky Terhune

Printed in Malaysia
1 3 5 6 4 2

SEP 2 6 2006		
OCT 0 4 REC'D		
NOV 2 7 2006		
NOV 1 3 REC'D		
DEC 0 3 2007		
NOV 2 0 REC'D		